Truth or Dare?

Helen Chapman

Editorial consultants:
Cliff Moon and Lorraine Petersen

RISING★STARS

Sch

nasen
NASEN House, 4/5 Amber Business Village, Amber Close,
Amington, Tamworth, Staffordshire B77 4RP

Rising Stars UK Ltd.
22 Grafton Street, London W1S 4EX
www.risingstars-uk.com

Text, design and layout © Rising Stars UK Ltd.
The right of Helen Chapman to be identified as the author of
this work has been asserted by her in accordance with the
Copyright, Design and Patents Act 1988.

Published 2007
Reprinted 2008 (twice)

Cover design: Button plc
Illustrator: Patrick Boyer
Text design and typesetting: Andy Wilson
Publisher: Gill Budgell
Commissioning editor: Catherine Baker
Publishing manager: Lesley Densham
Editor: Clare Robertson
Editorial consultants: Cliff Moon and Lorraine Petersen

British Library Cataloguing in Publication Data.
A CIP record for this book is available from the British Library

ISBN: 978-1-84680-206-5

Printed by Craft Print International Limited, Singapore

Contents

Characters

Declan   He's new to the school, but he's been on camp here before.

Zane   Zane is learning to skateboard.

Jack   Jack prefers to play safe.

Ben   He is good at skateboarding.

Mel   Like Ben, Mel likes a challenge.

Narrator   The narrator tells the story.

Scene 1

At the camp

Narrator	Declan is fed up with school camp. He doesn't know anyone. He wishes he was back at his old school. He is by himself, watching kids on their skateboards.
Ben	Zane, Jack, come here. If you want to see how to do a kick flip, watch Mel and me.
Zane	Sure. Thanks, Ben. I want to get it right for the King of Sports contest tomorrow.
Jack	Count me in. I keep falling off when I try to do a kick flip.

Ben   Stand on your board.

Mel   Like you're going to do an ollie.

Jack   Er – what's an ollie?

Mel   You know – when you pop
            the skateboard in the air?
            It looks like it's stuck to your feet.

Jack   Oh yes!

Ben   Hang your toes over the edge
            of your board.

Zane   Then what?

Ben   Put your back foot down.
            Bring your front foot over the side
            of the nose of your board.

Jack   Hang on! Which way do I look?
            Up or down or back or front?

Ben   It's up to you. When the board spins
            I think it helps to look at your back
            foot not your front foot.

Zane Then what?

Mel Then you land and roll away!

Jack Or fall off like I just did!
It's hard.

Ben Keep at it and you'll soon be
as good as me.

Mel And me!

Ben Just keep going and you'll be fine.

Declan Kick flips! Is that all you guys
can do? My six-year-old brother
can do better than that.

Ben What's it to you what we do?

Mel Yeah. I don't see you doing anything.
You're just standing there.

Narrator It's the first time anyone has talked to Declan all day.

Declan Yeah? Well that's because I don't want to do kids' stuff like you.

Jack We've only just started skateboarding, so back off.

Narrator Declan just grins at them.
He thinks getting on their nerves
is better than nothing.

Zane I bet you're all talk. I bet you can't do any tricks.

Declan I could if I wanted to.

Zane Go on then.

Mel Yeah, what are you waiting for, hot shot?

Ben He wants his mummy to hold his hand.

Declan   Hey, I can skateboard better than
you four put together. I can do loads
of tricks. Rock and roll, nose pick,
rocket air …

Jack   What's your name?

Declan   Declan.

Jack   Well Declan, look around.
You must see that we don't have
a ramp, or rails or jumps
or anything.

Zane   Even I know that you can't do tricks
like that here. All we've got is grass
and a dirt driveway full of holes.

Mel   There's no other place to ride.

Declan   Yes there is! I've been to this camp
with my last school. I know
a cool place.

Narrator   This is true. Declan does know
a cool place.

Declan   I skateboarded along the ledge
of a big hill. It was wicked.

Narrator   This is not true!
Liar, liar, pants on fire!

Ben   Show us then.

Mel   Yeah, come on, hot shot.

Narrator   Declan stops smiling.
Now he's got to show them.

Declan   Bring your boards.
We can ride some of the way.

Zane   What do you think, Jack?
             Do you want to go and see?

Jack   No, I'm going to stay here.

Ben   You've got to come, Jack.

Mel   Yeah, come on.
             Don't leave us stuck with Declan.

Zane   Come on, Jack, there's nothing
             else to do.

Jack   I want to do some more kick flips.
             I want to get as good as Ben and Mel.

Ben   Not going to happen, mate!
             We're just too good.

Jack   In your dreams!
             Okay, I give up.
             I'll come.

Narrator They all set off for the big hill.

Scene 2
Prove it

Narrator They ride their skateboards
in single file. Declan leads the way.

Mel This is taking forever.

Jack And we aren't meant to go off
on our own.

Zane I don't want to be late back
and miss dinner.

Ben Oi, Declan. Do you know
where you're going?

15

Declan   Of course I do. See that big green thing in front of us? It's called a hill. The ledge is on the hill and so that's why we're going towards it.

Jack   But it's too far away and I'm hot.

Declan   Look, I know I'm good, but even I can't make a hill come to me.

Ben   Are you sure this is the right way?

Narrator   Declan is *not* sure that this is the right way. The hill is easy to find but he is not so sure about the ledge. He knows that he will look really stupid if he gets everyone lost.

Jack   I can't skateboard any more, it's too bumpy.

Mel   Same here.

Zane   Looks as if we're all walking.

Jack   Let's go back.

Mel   What do you think, Ben?

Ben   I think he's making up this story
             about the ledge.
             Or trying to get us lost.

Narrator Declan gets off his skateboard.
             He puts it under his arm.
             He runs ahead and around
             a bend.

Zane   Where is he going?

Ben   I don't know, but I'm going
             after him.

Mel   Me too.

Jack   Don't. He's not worth it.

Zane   Come on, Jack; let's see what
he's up to.

Narrator   Mel and Ben run around
the bend and bump into Declan.

Declan   Hey, watch out!

Mel   So, hot shot, where's this
ledge then?

Declan   Look up. You can't miss it.

Narrator   The ledge sticks out from the rocks
on the hill. Jack and Zane come
round the bend. Together they
all stare at the ledge.

Declan   What do you think?

Narrator   The ledge looks bigger than
when Declan last saw it.
Not that he's going to tell
the others that. He grins at them.

Ben   There's no way you skateboarded
off that ledge.

Declan   Course I did. How many times
do I have to say it?

Mel   You can say it as many times
as you want to, but I still won't
believe you.

Declan   I tell you, I've been up there.

Zane   You couldn't have.
That ledge is too high up.

Declan   For you ladies maybe.
Not for me.

Ben   Prove it.

Declan   Why should I?

Zane   Because we don't believe you.

Mel   Yeah, prove it. I dare you.

Ben   I double dare you.

Jack   Okay guys, give it a rest.
Dares are stupid.

Mel   He won't do it. It's impossible,
like his story.

Declan   It isn't impossible!

Ben   It is!

Declan I'll show you. I'll take my
            skateboard up there now and …

Jack   Don't bother Declan.
            I believe you …

Declan It's too late. I never go back
            on a dare. But Ben and Mel
            have to do it too.
            If they can.

Ben   It looks very high.

Mel   And dangerous.

Declan   Now who's all talk?

Ben   No we're not.
We're as good as you.

Mel   No we're not.
We're better.

Jack   Can we go back now?
It's getting late.

Zane   No way, what about the dare?

Mel   Yeah, we want to see just how
good hot shot is.

Jack   But if he gets hurt he'll spend
the rest of camp in the sick bay.

Ben   And we won't have to put up
with him any more.

Declan   I'm going up.
See you losers later.

Ben   We'll be here watching everything
you do.

Mel   So don't even think of doing
anything sneaky.

Narrator But that's just what Declan *is* doing.

Scene 3
Hot cross bunny

Narrator Declan sets off. He is worried that if he loses the dare, no one will like him. Jack and Ben are worried too. If Declan does the dare, they'll be next.

Jack Is the climb as easy as it looks?

Declan It's not too bad. Doesn't help having my skateboard under one arm.

Zane I can see lots of footholds.

Declan I think this is where kids learn to rock climb.

Narrator Ben and Mel talk quietly together.

Ben Stop chewing your nails. It makes you look scared.

Mel I *am* scared! I'm good, but that ledge looks dangerous. Are you worried?

Ben Sort of. Don't tell the others, but I hate heights.

Mel What are we going to do?

Ben Hope that Declan bottles it.

Jack Did you hear that? It's the siren to go back to camp.

Mel If we're late for dinner we'll get into trouble.

Zane   And all the pizza will be gone.

Ben   Oi, Declan. Hurry up.

Declan   I'm going as fast as I can.

Narrator But Declan's plan is to go
very, very slowly. He knows that
a teacher will come looking
for them if they are late back.
She will make him come down
from the ledge. The dare
will be over.

Mel   Can anyone see him?

Ben   Nah, he must be behind a rock.

Zane   I like pizza. If we're late the meat
ones will be gone. I'll have to eat
ones with green stuff on them.

Mel   Don't forget they do a roll call too.
If we're not there, we're busted.

Jack   But we can't leave Declan.

Ben   I don't see what else we can do.

Narrator Declan has another plan.
This plan is better than his first one.
He calls to the others.

Declan   Hey, guys. I can see the camp
from up here. One of the teachers
is coming this way. You'd better
get going. If she finds you here
you'll be sent home.

Zane   I'm out of here. You heard
what Declan said. Don't forget
he was at the camp last year.

Mel   And don't forget we're in
the middle of a dare.

Jack   I don't care, I don't want to be
sent home. I'm going back too.

Narrator   Declan is really pleased. Things
are turning out even better
than he had planned. They fell
for his lie. Once they have gone
he can sneak down.

Ben   Jack, Zane, wait up you two.

Mel   Yeah, we've got to work out
what to do about Declan.

Narrator   The friends are busy talking.
Declan is sitting and watching them.
Suddenly, something nips his hand.

Declan   Ow! It bit me. A wild animal bit me.
I'll get mad cow disease!

Narrator   Declan leaps up in fright.

Declan   Get away from me.

Narrator   It's only a rabbit, but Declan
throws his skateboard at it.
The board misses the rabbit
and falls off the ledge.

Declan   Nooooo!

Narrator   Declan grabs at his skateboard.
He misses and falls over.

Declan   Ouch!

Narrator   He falls flat on his bum.

Declan   Oww!

Narrator   Then he slips and slides
down the hill and lands
with a thud.

Ben   What was that?

Jack   It must be Declan.

Mel   Yeah, turn around.
The hot shot has landed.

Zane   Has he done it? Has he really
skateboarded off the ledge?

Ben   He must have done.

Jack   He's hurt. He's got cuts and
            scratches all over him.

Zane   And blood.

Declan Hey guys! Am I King of the Hill
            or what?

Mel   Yeah, you did okay.

Declan Okay? No, I was wicked.

Jack   But you got hurt.

Declan I landed badly. My foot got
            stuck between my skateboard
            and the ground.

Zane   And where's your skateboard?

Mel   Here it is, stuck in a bush.

Zane   We need to get back, now!

Declan Hang on, what about the dare?

Narrator   Ben and Mel wish Camp was over –
and the stupid dare. But it isn't.

Ben   We'll do it tomorrow.

Mel   Yeah, and then you won't be
the only King of the Hill.

Scene 4
Kings of the Hill

Narrator The next morning, Ben and Mel climb to the ledge.

Jack Good luck!

Zane Be careful.

Narrator Ben and Mel get on their skateboards.

Ben I want to get this over with. I'll go first, okay?

Mel Yeah, I'm cool.

Ben Here goes.

Mel   You're standing wrong.

Ben   I know. Being so high up
is freaking me out.

Mel   I'll go first and you follow me down.

Narrator   Mel starts off, but the speed wobbles
set in. She stays safe by doing
a back flip over the skateboard
and jumping off.

Jack   What's going on?

Zane   I'm not sure.

Declan Those guys are such losers.

Narrator   Jack calls up to the ledge.

Jack   Ben, what's happening?

Ben   Er … quite a lot. Mel went
                one way and her skateboard
                went another way.

Zane   And?

Mel   I landed on Ben and
                we fell down.

Jack   Are you hurt?

Ben   Just sore.
                But there's a big problem.
                Parts of the ledge have broken off.

Mel   And we're stuck out on the end.

Zane   Can't you get back the way
                you came?

Ben   No. If we move, the rest
                of the ledge might break.

Declan   What about the dare?
              Why don't you skateboard down?

Ben   We can't reach our boards.

Jack   I'll get a teacher.

Mel

Zane

              } No!

Ben

Declan

Ben   You'll get us into trouble.

Jack   You're already in trouble.

Mel   But we can sort it out
              on our own.

Zane   Declan, you can help
              bring them down.

Jack   Yes, you've been up there.
              Twice!

Declan I don't know …
I don't think I can.

Narrator Declan looks up at Ben and Mel.
Their faces are white.
He has to do something.

Declan Hold on, I'm coming to get you.
I'll bring you back down.

Narrator Declan climbs until he is under
the ledge.

Declan Ben, you've got to get over
the ledge.

Ben I can't. I'll fall.

Declan No you won't.

Mel It's okay, Ben.
I've got your hands.

Narrator Slowly, Ben backs over the side
of the ledge.

Zane Look, I can see him.

Jack His legs are dangling in the air.
I can't watch.

Declan Ben, let go. The drop's only a metre
or so.

Narrator Ben drops onto the rock.

Mel Look out! Here I come.

Declan Now, I'm going to talk
you guys down.

Zane If they slip it's a long way down.

Declan Move your left foot down a bit,
Ben. That's it. That's a foothold.

Ben Now what?

Declan Keep moving. Mel, you follow Ben.
There are lots of footholds here,
the worst is over.

Narrator Ten minutes later, all three
of them are back on the ground.

Zane Am I glad to see you.

Jack That was awesome, Declan.

Mel Yeah, you really are a hot shot.

Ben You won the dare.
You're the King of the Hill.

Declan No, I'm not.

Ben What do you mean?
You won the dare.

Mel Yeah, you skateboarded off the ledge.

Declan No I didn't. I faked it.

Jack What?

Zane   You're kidding us, right?

Declan   No.

Ben   So you made us go up there
and we didn't have to?

Mel   Wow! You must really hate us.

Declan   No I don't. I really like you guys.
The whole dare thing just got a bit
out of hand. I'm sorry.

Jack   But we saw you climb on to the ledge.

Zane   And we saw you when you came down.

Ben   You couldn't have faked it.
We'd have seen you.

Mel   And you were so fast.

Declan   I was fast because I fell.
A wild animal spooked me.
I threw my skateboard at it.

Jack   You're lying again.
What wild animal?

Declan   Um … a rabbit.

Zane   You are kidding?

Declan   No, it was big with sharp teeth.

Zane   A bunny rabbit?
You total wuss, Declan.

Jack   But it took guts going up to help
Ben and Mel.

Ben   I think you are the King of the Hill.

Mel   Me too!

Declan   No, I reckon we three are *all*
Kings of the Hill.

Zane   And Jack and me will be
King of Sports this afternoon.

Mel   How do you work that out?

Jack   You three can't enter. Declan's
skateboard is a write-off.
And yours and Ben's are still
on the hill!

Drama ideas

After Scene 1

- What do you think will happen next?
  Will Declan try to get out of
  skateboarding on the ledge?
  Or will he do it?

- Talk about this in your group,
  and act out your ideas.

After Scene 2

- With a partner, be Jack and Mel.
- Jack should tell Mel why he thinks
  dares are stupid, and Mel should
  tell Jack why she thinks they
  are good.

2

After Scene 3

- Hotseating: choose one person to be Declan.

- Everyone else can ask Declan questions to find out why he behaves the way he does in the play. Is he hoping to make the others be friends with him?

After Scene 4

- In your group, act out a scene from later in the camp.

- Your scene can show whether Declan makes friends with the others or not.

RISING STARS

PHONE
0871 47 23 010

www.risingstars-uk.com